The
LAST CANDLES

The LAST CANDLES

Tony Curtis

SEREN BOOKS
*1989

SEREN BOOKS is the book imprint of
Poetry Wales Press Ltd.,
Andmar House, Tondu Road, Bridgend,
Mid Glamorgan

© Tony Curtis, 1989

British Library Cataloguing in Publication Data

Curtis, Tony, *1946–*
  The last candles.
  I. Title
  821'.914

  ISBN 1-85411-005-5
  ISBN 1-85411-006-3 paperback

All rights reserved. No part of this publication may be
reproduced, stored in a retrieval system, or transmitted in
any form or by any means, electronic, mechanical,
photocopying, recording or otherwise, without the prior permission
of the copyright holder.

*The publisher acknowledges the financial support of the
Welsh Arts Council*

Cover drawing: Charles Burton

Typeset in 11 point Palatino
by Megaron, Cardiff
Printed and bound in Great Britain at
The Camelot Press plc, Southampton

Contents

I

9 Midnights
10 Games With My Daughter
11 The Nurse
12 The Mower
13 Making Bread for *Sunblest*
14 The Loft
17 Great Uncle Charlie 1893-1986
20 Leaks
21 Annie
23 Fisher
24 Painting Him Out
26 Public Sale: Andrew Wyeth
27 Wind From The Sea
28 The Gulf Stream
30 Villanelle for a Photographer
31 Sick Child
32 Maquette
33 The Immortality of Birds

II

37 Thoughts from the Holiday Inn

III

49 Summer in Greece
50 Poles

51 Kalavryta
52 Window Seat to Chicago
53 Witness
56 Barry Island Dream
58 Breaking Surface
60 The Emerald
62 At Ochrid Lake
64 From the City that Shone
66 The Last Candles
69 Friedhof
71 Home Front
73 Couples from the Fifties
75 Hotel Carmarthen
77 To Arthur
79 Train Journey: Triangles
81 After Skopje
83 The Treble
85 Second Half

I

MIDNIGHTS

An ice wind from the east razors across
the water, heaves and slams up our road. All night
our windows flinch and rattle with bitter complaints,
for hours the roof lifts and the attic breathes.

In the morning the last of our apples lie
bounced and bruised beneath the trees,
our front cherry's bare as a plucked chicken,
leaves downed across the lawn, its carcass full of sky.

A handful of slates, as old as the century
have snapped and slid to crash the sloping
panes of the verandah — slivers and blades
of glass in the flower border like dew glistening.

I bend for an hour over the job, filling
a bucket with needles, jags and shards.
This evening the weather man promises calm,
explains, last night's storm was brewed in Poland,

a wind from Warsaw chilling across the continent to Wales.
We hold to each other now
and listen to nothing but midnight
taxis speeding out of town.

As I stroke your arm
a glass sliver still in my finger
bloodies the two of us.
The windows' thin moonlight fails.

GAMES WITH MY DAUGHTER

The first clear afternoon of Spring bursts
April's buds and bulbs in the park.
This year when I catch and take her weight
she powers the swing and arcs
from finger-stretch behind my head
to soaring feet-in-the-clouds.
Mothers to our left and right
shrink in their corridors of safe flight.

Our game's revealed the filling out,
the firmer, young woman's stare,
the promise Winter concealed beneath its coat.
Forward and up she splits the sky, each
swing down and back she goes by to where
my tip-toed fingers' grasp can't reach.

THE NURSE

wakes us at seven.
My hand shuffles around your breast,
your snore whistles down into breath.
The lamp blasts on,
a pencil thermometer pushes between my lips,
tastes like lead under the tongue.
My dream turns to
rooks on a church roof, flowers
bent in a stone vase.

Two notepapers in the shape of hearts —

pulse thick

sleep calm

We insist,
"We are well. Go back to bed.
We are cured. You did it.
You are the doctor.
Let us sleep now."

It's too early, much too early
for t.v. for Sunday love-making.
For the insistent nurse
who wants to play and will not,
cajoled or bribed by anything but love,
will not go away.

THE MOWER

Each autumn I forget to oil it,
forget to clean the blade
and keep a wash of petrol in the tin.

My father would have given that knowing look
and lectured me on caring.
When the evenings drain away

I slam shut the shed door
against winter, leaving spring
to work its own passage.

And now the lawn's a mess, wants cutting,
I find the blade dull and caked,
the handle's grown more rust.

Still, a sly kick, a curse
and the pull-slop, pull-slop of the cord
jerk-starts summer into noise.

That first run the length of the lawn,
the first breath of exhaust and grass
grown sappy and prime —

this is the time that sets another year bleeding.

MAKING BREAD FOR *SUNBLEST*

To be with you
all that summer vacation
I made bread for *Sunblest* in north Wales.
Not so much a bakery, more a bread factory
with conveyor-belt proving of the machined dough,
conveyor-belt ovens where we stood all night
in the river of loaves, catching
the burning tins in our mittens
with awkward puppet-grasps and banging
the crisp ochre bricks out
on to the cooling racks. A crew
of students mucking in with the old hands,
men who'd been, in their time, real bakers,
moving now like automatons through the early hours.

And in the meal-breaks I'd strip
my white overalls to run the mile
to your house, scratch at your father's back-door:
a cup of tea from your mother, served discreetly,
away in the kitchen while the old man
glowered at his blaring t.v.
You'd walk me back to the gate, chilled in the air
and still flour-dusty for the jog back under
the stars. We'd kiss.
Across twenty years these things
return, distracting me tonight
as I rise, proving constant
in your practised hands.

THE LOFT

I've made up me mind.
I'm packing the birds in,
the loft can go.
There's too much to do,
in the house, like,
and outside. The lawn takes two
hours cutting, and the veg garden
... what do I want with all that veg?
There's company down the club, I know,
but I can't hear with that organ
going down there. The smoke
gets so bad you can't breathe.

No, I'll pack it in
back end of this year,
though I'm cock of the club this season —
Old Bird Average, Cross-Channel, Best Young Bird,
Gloucester Annual. I said
to them, give me one cup, like, one
big cup. Last season we had a box full
of them replicas — the case in there
won't take no more.
Where would I put them all?

Your mother used to clean them.
They used to shine.

Did she ever tell you how we met?
Knocked each other over in an air-raid.
I chased her up from seeing her uniform
and next day I took a lorry

and drove across to the hospital and parked
right outside and was meself chased
off by this matron — a real dragon she were,
*I won't have the likes of soldiers
pestering my girls*, she said.
Forty years ago and more.
Brought together we was by the war.

I sold a good 'un this week.
Eight years a winner,
from a class sire and grandame,
his sons and daughters all winners.
I sold him back to the bloke that bred him.
Could have fetched a bit in the auction
— a hundred pounds or more.
Sold it back for thirty quid.
For stock.

Yes, it's been one of me best years.
I had one back the other week been
missing for two months. This lad sent
thirty-two birds to the same race
and never seen a feather, not a feather.
One of the top fanciers in the Fed.
A big crash it were, over the Channel from France.

That bird of mine come back like a good 'un.
From the East Coast, I shouldn't wonder.
Walked it. Picking grain
from the fields and making
his way all the time. They can

do that with it being harvest time,
barley crops mostly. They drop
and eat what's left. Course, then
he has to line himself up again.

No, I've had enough. There's too much to do.
Monday, I cleaned the cooker. Took me a good hour.
Under the rims, the grill-pan, all over.
Tuesday, I did the beds ready for you.
It's too much looking after the loft.

Your mother used to make me a cup
when I was watching out for them
and she'd help me, remember,
bring 'em down and clock 'em in.
It's the time on the clock that counts.
Could be split seconds between winning
and nothing.

A year it'll be, next month.
In November.

GREAT UNCLE CHARLIE 1893–1986

What better way to end it all
than this January day,
the fields across to Peasmore fresh with rain
and Enbourne's church, St Michael
and All Angels held in seven centuries of air;
the grave's sides of polished Berkshire clay?

Now the month-old holly lies in our hearth,
spikes curled and brown,
but the berries' fire still glows
red as the poppy in his wreath.

The last time we saw him alive
a week before Christmas,
was in the cottage hospital flanked
by two of the dying, the obviously dying,
his mouth slack and eyes closed
until our voices woke him
and he smiled. His eyes brightened
and widened under the full, white head of hair.
He shook our hands, that odd
grip with two finger-ends lost
in the press at Simpson's the printers
where he'd been apprenticed as a lad.
Pronounced unfit with a dicky heart
for Haig's trenches, he'd lived
to see this century to its last gasp.

For an hour and a half he kept us talking,
flirting with a nurse, joking with the tea-lady.
Then I brought him round to the war:

*They chose me from the ambulance men
and had me dressed in full uniform
to drive the old King to Reading,
to the station where they brought the wounded in.
Rows and rows of stretchers along the platform.
And a band playing full blast.
Old George, he stopped every yard or so,
and some of 'em* (and here Charlie lowered his voice
in deference to those dying at his sides)
had no . . . (he touched his arm) *and some of 'em
no* . . . (and here his leg). *An' you know
what his majesty said — he said, "Don't
you worry, my man (and most of 'em were
no more than boys) don't you worry," he said,
"we shall soon have you back and fighting the Hun."*

Charlie's eyes focussed away to the far wall.
*One morning Mrs Cooper at Thatcham
lost all three of her sons.
Same morning.
On the Somme.*

*Before driving back we took
armfuls of ripe holly from his tree
at the backdoor.*
                      *D'you know
how that tree came to be here?
One day I left my spade in the earth
and a robin perched there.*

That holly was no higher than myself
and just out of shot as we posed for family snaps
— Uncle and Dad and Mum and Gran and me
pulling at my slack bow and arrow.
My father's jacket bulging with coins,
keys, tobacco, just like Charlie's,
his hand gripping a pipe, the other
clenched in his pocket, just like Charlie's.

Great Uncle Charlie,
you survive all the characters.
I place you at the wheel of a Ford Pop.
chugging to the top of the Air-Balloon.
Perched on that hill like a climber
looking back towards Berkshire,
you're rubbing tobacco in your palm,
packing it down in the bowl as if those finger
-stumps had been fashioned for the act.
The match flares for a moment
and the smoke catches in a wind that
twists it up and over your face. From below
it seems, almost, a halo.

LEAKS

The balcony window frames Martyn and Son
who balance on stilts to fix a length of gutter.
On the sick? he asked
when I answered his knock in my dressing-gown.
So now, rinsed of sleep and dressed,
I assume my serious gaze into the screen,
wishing my keys clacked like an ancient Remington,
a real writer's machine, or that, through the open doors
my creased brow would creak its concentration
above their hammers' attention to repair and order.

Today's sky is an overture to Winter.
All through the rough months the water
now will funnel from our roof to flow
obediently down the sealed gutter.
Dry, away from the weather breaking at our bows,
I'll sit at this desk, blocked, staring out
beyond the green lichen of words this screen grows,
and watch the rain compose *andantes* on the slate.
The sky defining edge and slope of the roof,
firmly, as if a hand held a palette knife.

ANNIE

If there is witchcraft, let it be this:
Aunt Annie seen first through the split
windscreen of our Morris Minor beetling
down the twisting lane to her cottage,
and Annie at the clothes-line hanging what
seemed to be a long belt or strap but
which proved to be an adder's skin she'd
stripped from the creature discovered
in her strawberry-patch, trapped
under her metal-shod clog and dispatched
with the head of her rake.

What kind of trophy that was,
whether powdered spine or dried blood
helped in the charming of warts or tumours,
or whether she cast that snake into the pot
as the gypsies did, I'll not speculate over
this length of years, but her collie Scamp,
a yapping familiar, leapt at our tyres
as we entered the brambly yard
and rooks rose from their tree-colony in warning
as if we had discovered some lurking thing
the gypsy moor and woods held secret.

Annie would rough-tongue me for a watery town boy,
spoiled by lean bacon, soft eggs and sugar-cube oranges:
I plunged her in the sorcerer's cauldron
and broomsticked her from my weekend dreams.
Monthly we'd have her up in town to visit
her Ginnie, a poor, wild thing held in St. David's
up on the hill for her own good, who raved and punched

the air, mad with her shrunken world and all of us beyond
I knew her through family whispers, nods and winks,
a nightmare, unfocussed by face or dress
and free to float through bedroom walls.

Years later, with my own hostages cast to fortune,
I learned from a chance remark my mother made
that Ginnie, now long dead, had been
no thrown-off daughter sent by Annie to the discretion
of the madhouse: but her sister's child, pushed
out of shame, out of the county,
out of sight and mind.
They'd find her wandering on the Tenby road,
laughing at the day-trip charabancs,
kneeling in ditches with her hands
cupped in the muddy flow, panning the sun's gold.

On one visit Annie, a widow and childless,
died in our house, ugly to the last.
So I turned away and she was spirited
downstairs and out of our lives.
I remember no funeral.
Pembrokeshire Charmers pass the healing gift
from female to male, male to female.
The Bible verses, wild garlic, thyme,
chicken's feet, whatever she practised,
tricks or gift, vanished with her last pinched breath.
If that was witchcraft it was a small thing,
a bunched grasp of herbs and words and a wishing
that now I begin to understand, and could learn to take
like a child reading an S, seeing a snake.

FISHER

With my second it was different.
One morning I heard him come in
and I knew something was up.
Since he lost his work he'd been down.
I couldn't do anything.
He was in the front room
with the tele on straight away.
Want a cup? I said.
He just stared.
Don't just sit there I said
If you're home you can see to the fish.
He didn't move a muscle.

I was ironing when I heard the crash.
He'd smashed the glass with his fist.
Holding the heater with both burnt hands
he was and blood
from his wrists all over the table.
You've never seen such a mess —
water and blood across the carpet
weeds, gravel, and the fish flapping
and jumping, their little tails
and eyes going wild —
mollies and guppies and platties
red-eyes, pink-kissers —
the bloody lot.

Jesus I said.
I remember.
He said
save them

PAINTING HIM OUT

That morning she drew back the curtains
on the promise of sun.
Now she would do it.
The brush nuzzled into the creamy tin.
Starting at the top left-hand corner
she spread the colour
so it licked over and in
to the skin of the paper,
salving the scuffs and fadings,
soothing the bruised angles and corners.
Though at each finishing stroke
the bristles razored the edged crack
between paper and wood, the hairs growing spiked
and stubborn as his with sweat after running
or love. The handle moistening in her hand,
she worked with a rhythm, giving
herself to each wall in turn,
three times until it was done.

The chair she stood upon is starred by flecks
and the whorls of her finger-prints.
The old sheets rolled away, the brush
loosening its load and softening under the tap water.
She climbs the stairs again and the sun
which had risen behind her back,
through the day lighting over her shoulder
her work, has fallen to the gable-end
and now side-lights the view from her french-windows,
applying a wash over the town, the pink-brown sea,
across to a muted, distant coastline

where, she knows, he will be
driving, or eating, or laughing
in different colours.

PUBLIC SALE: ANDREW WYETH

This selling is a wake.
Neighbours and friends gather at the end of it all
and young folks setting up for themselves,
putting good use to the bargains
from another man's loss.
The rusting Ford tractor, a plough, bales
of wire and fence posts, the bowl
she baked with, the goat that nuzzled
her skirt where the chicken feed
had stained. On mornings such as this,
the blue-grey sky flat as an iron,
she laid her corn mosaic across the yard
and watched the hens pick it clean away.

Man can't manage without a wife.

Evening after evening
still the sun reddened over the hill.
Now it was cheese and store bread, eggs
smashed into the pan. The strange feel
of his hands softening in the sink water.
He'd shutter the windows and turn
to the cold bed. Scared of those nights,
but lost in the break of morning.

When a man's left alone, seems like
his fields pull further towards the sky-line,
the earth fights harder against the plough.

One by one their laden trucks leave,
churning the dirt road into furrows
that a man could plant so easily.

WIND FROM THE SEA

a villanelle for Andrew Wyeth

Wind from the sea
Takes the stale net curtain in its teeth
And the shreds stream away from me.

The woven birds caught in its vagary
Are lifted and shaken by the force beneath
Wind from the sea.

The frayed curtain composes a plea —
Men o' War blossom like sailors' wreaths
And the shreds stream away from me;

The torn lace prints a skeleton tree
Against grey skies that drown belief.
Wind from the sea

Lances over the forest of pines, see —
It drives and cuts without relief
And the shreds stream away from me.

Stand at the window, stare to infinity,
What's promised will prove the leavings of a thief —
Wind from the sea —
And the shreds stream away from me.

THE GULF STREAM

The black man by Winslow
Homer is still
a negro.

Exhausted, strapped to the deck,
his head turns to gauge
the distance of the twister
spiralling like a child's top
from the grey horizon.
Bow-sprit and mast splintered,
rigging shredded, he is doomed.
The three huge sharks snapping
wildly through flotsam
are hardly necessary
except that this is art
not life.

The black man
by Winslow Homer
is still a negro.

Muscular, ebony,
his head turned resolutely
(not as I had thought to the tornado)
but away from all the action —
the sharks, the wreckage of his boat;
and that distant three-master
full-sailed, busy in its own sea,
speeding across an opaque horizon.
Stoic, sole survivor,
he has his own vision.

We are satisfied knowing
he sees something we
could never see.

(And this was painted in
the nineteenth century.)

VILANELLE FOR A PHOTOGRAPHER

O. Winston Link: *Hot Shot East at Iaeger,*
West Virginia, August 1956

The smooching couple in the chrome saloon
Are teasing love in their fumbling way
As the Norfolk & Western steams before an August moon.

On the drive-in screen a wounded MIG plumes
Through a cold-war sky. Strategic blunders will betray
The smooching couple in the chrome saloon.

Whose earnest gropings, sighs and moans
Counterpoint the loco's thrust and sway
As the Norfolk & Western steams before an August moon.

Link's wired-up lamps, set to jewel the gloom,
Flashlight the upholstered Fifties and display
The smooching couple in the chrome saloon.

What gung-ho promise drowns in a Korean monsoon
While marines act out some crude screenplay?
As the Norfolk & Western steams before an August moon,

Like train-crossed lovers in a soft-top tomb,
These clean-cut kids compose their dream, in a Chevrolet,
The smooching couple in the chrome saloon
As the Norfolk & Western steams before an August moon.

SICK CHILD

Red-haired Sophie
Pillowed in bed, wrecked
Against the headboard.

Caught in the undertow of a treacherous tide,
Her blood swirls in a wash of the sea.
Tuberculosis has scoured her out like a shell.

At the bedside her mother sits doubled
With the ache of certain loss,
Her face bleared into her chest.

She holds to Sophie, fingers curled so firmly, so long
Around fingers that the knuckles are flushed red
Like rocks poised for the sky's spilling of dawn.

Frail anemone the child against the coral pillow,
Weed-green the bedcover,
Driftwood the table and cupboard.

The mother's tight, black hair is tied and twisted back,
Her body curled and falling in a slow
Black wave over a deep rock.

Munch

MAQUETTE

The dancer is poised to fly
the arrow of himself into
all of space beyond.
Wild Nijinski's a taut bow
notched by the fingers of the old artist,
that large and lively greybeard.

He pauses in the late afternoon,
turning his back on the maquette,
the study photographs from the ballet,
and wipes his fingers of the clay.
At the door of the bedroom a hand enters,
lightly touches the frame, then (perhaps)

beckons. He follows,
to worship at the temple, he says.
Nijinsky is held to the instant of movement
and holds and holds, while the wise
old hands, smelling like a gardener's,
work at her (almost) perfect breast.

Rodin

THE IMMORTALITY OF BIRDS

The great man talked at length
but slowly, and with long pauses
in which his eyes closed, as if
viewing the moments he would call up into words.

In one of those pauses his eyes
fluttered at a sound from behind his head —
his caged bird fell silent, then dead from its perch
landing with a soft finality.

Madam raised a finger to beckon
his chauffeur and dresser. This young man
left the room and we heard the Mercedes growl
its way down the twists of their hill.

Pablo continued: *I remember
the clean blue of the ocean that summer* . . .
the walnuts ripened early that year . . .
The car returned and the driver entered unseen.

He stretched his hand into the cage
to catch the dead linnet in his fingers
and release from his palm, like a magician,
a new singing bird bought from the village.

Ah! the old man said, licking his dry mouth,
*paintings may grow tired and fade
but an artist is truly chosen
whose birds sing eternally. Listen!*

II

THOUGHTS FROM THE HOLIDAY INN

for John Tripp

"When you're dead, you're bloody dead."
We both liked the punch of that one, John, said
Ten or more years ago by an author breaking
Through his fiction, kicking the rules, risking
All our willing disbelief to shock through
To the truth. B.S. Johnson, that sad and tortured man, knew
The whole thing to be by turns a joke, by turns the need
To love each other into something close to sense. We bleed,
John, we bleed, and time bleeds from our wrists.
Your death was shocking, and tidies up another lovely, angry
    (when pissed),
Poet of a man, who would not, for anyone, be tidied into
    respectability
Longer than an evening, or his allotment in some anthology.
There's too much to be said, by too many, too soon.
But from this lunchtime watering place, this unlikeliest of rooms,
Spare me the modest time and space — by Christ, you've enough
Of both in death old mate — to work things out, sound off —
About the months you've missed, the months that we've missed you.
You'd have seen this place go up, the skyline that you knew
Transformed, jagged, blocked as urban planners brought rationality
To what the coal century had grown and shaped to the Taff's
    estuary.
We've needed you here, John, thrusting out your neck and
    stroking the chin
From a classy, fraying shirt to show the disdain we hold these
    people in,
These late-comers to a country and a nation in a mess.
They've given us the bum's rush today, John, I must confess.
We checked out the place for next year's Literature Festival

And sponsorship. As far as we could tell
It was a waste of time, for any management
Who'd given Sickle-Cell Research the thumbs down were clearly bent
On profit, and to hell with charity, never mind cultural P.R.
Well fed and disappointed, we returned to the bar.
Still, they'd named the two big function rooms, the 'Dylan Suite'
And 'Gwyn Jones Room'. "Don't know him," said the manageress,
    with complete
Honesty. "He's one of our Academy's most distinguished senior
    members,"
I said, and thought, We do no more than blow upon the embers,
We scribblers who'd want to claim
That everything in Wales for praise or blame
Is brought to life and fact and mythical creation
By that writerly mix of ego and the grasp of a tradition.
What use we prove, the weight the world gives us, if any,
Is likely to be cheap and grudging, no more than a blunt penny
Flung to shut our mannered, metred whining.
Then, later, taken up again shining
From the rubbing our tongues and lives impart.
I hear you answer, John, "It's a start, boy, some sort of bloody start."
John, further down the Hayes, now I think of you, haunting those
    benches
And passing a coffee or the length of a fag below the rich stenches
From Brains's brewery snugged in behind the Royal Arcade.
As the big internationals move in and build and build the shade
And sunlight shift position down the city's roads.
In spruced-up Bute (re-named, as Tiger Bay encodes
A docklands past we'd best forget or sanitise
In tarted-up pubs or tree-lined low-rise
Flats — *The Jolly Tar* or *Laskar's Close*)

The men who clinch the deals, the gaffers, the boss
With the tax-free Daimler, the Series Seven,
Square out the mazy city into real estate concepts, proven
Returns for their money. They are gilt-edged applicants
For Euro-funds, Welsh Development grants.
This hotel is for the likes of them. It stretches eye to eye
With the brewery's silver funnel, two hundred bedrooms in the sky
Starting at fifty quid the night. "Fat cats," I hear you say
"And that's before your breakfast. Stuff the fucking pool. O.K."
Tax payer's rage? John, even you, an occasional connoisseur
Of hotel fitments and glimpses of the soft life, would incur
A gullet-sticking at this pricey junk, mock-Grecian style
Arches, columns, thick marble-facings done in tiles,
Plush, deep divans around an open fire beneath a metal canopy,
Surrogate logs you'd hardly warm your hands upon. You'd see
Beyond, the indoor pool, functional, gaunt,
More marble, sharp angles with, each end, broken columns to flaunt
The facile version of classic decor money'll buy
And set down in a city anywhere, across a sky
Or ocean. Continent to continent there must be travellers
Who need the reassurance of such nondescript pools and bars,
To step off the plane or train, taxi down concrete tracks
To what the Telex reservation guarantees predictable: stacks
Of credit-cards accepted, pool-side temperature just O.K.
An in-house movie they choose and relay
To each room in American or English — God forbid
The native patois — (*These people down here, the Welsh — did
You say — a language all their own — an ancient tongue?
— King Arthur — well, I saw a movie when I was a kid, sung
The songs all that summer — Dannie Kay — got it!*)
John, what kind of progress is all this shit?

They took the coal-miners and put 'em in a coal museum:
And the people drove down, coughed up three quid ten just to
    see 'em.
Tourists one-nighting en route the Beacons, Bath or Ireland:
"Cardiff — what's that?" "The airport . . . it's halfways there. I
    planned
To break the trudge from Heathrow." And what of the locals?
Lunchtimes bring yuppies of both sexes, the gals
Waft in like *Cosmo* covers, the men have knife-
Creased casuals, hook their index fingers through the keyrings of life.
And there's the mid-day nibblers, women past their prime
But dressed to the nines and painted, passing the time
Between Howells' upholstery and Hones and Jones with a small gin
And sandwich triangles of horseradish and smoked salmon,
Piquant, hardly fattening. Their cigarette smoke curls
Away with the suggestion of rope, these former good-lookers, girls
Who, thirty years before, bagged a man of promise or means
And moved up, to Cyncoed, out to Lisvane, a pool, lawns
Done by a man who brings his own machine and strips
His shirt in the long afternoons. They tip
Him with the last cut of September.
Their husbands are on the board and successfully bored.
    "Remember,"
They'd say, "when we had that little detached in Newport,
And we'd spend Sundays, you mowing and me trimming." "I've
    fought
Hard to get this far, and Christ, there's times I wonder,
What for? What have we got? Where's it gone? Just blunder
On to the next rung, dinner party, contract, barbeque."
"Love, you're working too hard. Is the company proving too
    much for you?"

John, excuse this indulgence, that clumsy fiction, it's no digression,
I'm still concerned to understand progression.
When working-class is all you've known
These rich fish cruise by bright-coloured (if overblown)
Distracting — but these too are tenants of the pool
You plunged your wit and pen into. Fool
No-one was your aim, and at last came the anger of *Life Under
    Thatcher.*
But winos in the Hayes betray a watcher
Who'd sum up the whole state of things in verses.
It's too easy to shoot off steam in curses
That pepper the mark but fail to penetrate.
Guys with real assets, clever portfolios, are immune to street hate;
They justify themselves in terms of respectability, vision,
    advancement.
The world's an oyster if you lift your nose off the pavement.
They've bought themselves out of the firing line.
Windows purr close, revs slipping the motor into fifth gear, it feels
    fine
To loosen out along the motorway — weekends in Pembs
Or, turning right, over the Bridge, a trim two hours to dine by the
    Thames.
No-one's rooted anymore, John, as you must have known —
"The old man" coming to smith in Taffs Well in the '3Cs where
    you'd grown
Up Welsh, not Cornish like him, in all but the language.
(The wounding of that loss, it seems, no achievements can assuage.)
And, because of that, confused, determined and concerned
As the rest of us, excluded from the *Gorsedd* but feeling you'd
    earned
The right to sound off for this Wales — Taffs and Gwerin,

To voice the peculiar place of the eighty per cent. The din
Of justified protest settled after '79 — Welsh cheque books,
    Channel Four.
The nationalist drummings the Sixties saw you working for
You realised later were too easy, too raw. Like R.S.
You loved the country with a passion, an anger, but the less
Misty, period-costume work will surely prove the best,
The more enduring; real poetry "welcoming the rough-weather
    guest".
John, I would rather have seen your ashes ebb from Barafundle
Bay. That grey day at Thornhill we watched your coffin trundle
Behind the curtains to the kind of anonymity
You'd rail against for other "botched angels", losers we
Turn away from, society's mistakes, the hard-done-to,
Underdogs you wanted to feel close to.
The glow of a cupped-hand fag was light enough to draw
You to some alley, a derelict huddled there against a door,
One of the Hollow Men, a voter with no vote
Wrapped in old woollens, *Echoes* stuffed inside an overcoat.
"Cold enough, butt, eh? on the street. Here, have yourself a cuppa.
Take care, old fella, and watch out for the copper.
Those bastards aren't for the likes of us,
They don't give a tinker's cuss
As long as things stay down and quiet, and everything's neat.
You and me'll keep to the shadows, butt, and stay light on our
    feet."
I've a feeling poetry's not the thing most apt
To dissect society, or politicise an audience one imagines trapped
In wilful ignorance, lobotomised by the trashy press,
Disenfranchised by the soapy box, seduced by the caress
Of the goodish life in the second half of this softening century.

You, fellow sprinter, took your chance through readings — could be
Five or fifty listeners, in club. gallery, college, school.
But articles in the London nationals, plays on the t.v. as a rule
Work most action, albeit short-lived. We
Poets light shower-burning fuses or rockets you see
Flash and quickly fade as the moment's charged
And spent. John, you saw the first decade of this city enlarged,
Pulled into the dream-shape someone thought we needed.
At fifty-nine who's to say you'd not changed things, not succeeded
In stirring up whatever stuff this corner of the pool had in
    suspension?
Talk of booze, too little care taken of yourself, prevention
Of the heart's explosion that took you in the early hours
With McGuigan's fight won and the tele drizzling showers
Of grey flakes down its mute screen,
Won't bring you back. You slid away. The barely-tuned machine
Packed up. Unlike Dylan, no insult to the brain, John. Often we'd talk
Of going to the States, whistle-stopping, the Chelsea in New York,
Our tour for the Yanks, I could have rigged.
Yes, if I'd pushed it, we two in tandem could have gigged
Over there. Like a lot of the others, I chickened out, I suppose.
Pembrokeshire a couple of nights — you with no change of clothes,
Just a battered attaché, poems, toothbrush, fags —
Was the limit of my stamina for your ways. Memory drags
Such petty guilts to the fore.
Though I treasure and feed off that reading we did on the man o' war,
Reluctant sailors pouring export ale down us
To forestall the poetry (they did) drown us
With hospitality in the middle of Fishguard harbour
Until we staggered past the missiles in her belly's store
Up to the frigate's redundant forward gun-turret, officers dressed

In cummerbunds, and elegant women. The talk was veiled, but
    impressed
Words like 'Responsibility', 'Capability' and 'Global role'. "Yes, but
What do you do with all this training? All the missiles, shit-hot
Fire-power?" I remember, he answered you with, "We can blow
    Fishguard
Away with each one, you know. We are, I suppose, a 'hard
Fist gloved by our democratic masters'." John, before the evening
    ended
You topped that with a poem scribbled on a cigarette pack. We
    descended
A precarious ladder to the launch with those lines of his and yours
    sinking
Into the night. And now, a decade later, the story has a ring
Any writer could tune. Perhaps that's what your Sandeman Port
    inquisitor
Pointed to — after the jaunts and applause, the writer's for
Filling the void, putting structure into space, a kind of race
Against apathy and oblivion. Too grand, you say, too heroic? Let's
    face
It, John, we've both indulged in our 'intervals of heat'
On the page and off. Both been chilled by the thought one couldn't
    beat
The odds — stuck in Wales, chiselling verse, weak in the flesh.
We're out on the edge of the world's concern, no Wall St, no
    Long Kesh.
Unless the challenge here is also to connect — radar dishes at
    Brawdy,
Hinkley over the water, Trawsfynydd, the poison brought in on our
    sea.
An *Anglo*, dipped in England's sewer should still produce the goods.

Albeit in "invisible ink / on dissolving paper . . ." one loads
The futile quarto, pushes it out to travel or sink.
Standing here before the Holiday Inn, and its shiny 0-3-0, I think
How my grandfather, before the Great War, shunted down to Wales
    on the G.W.R.
How arbitrary one's identity is: with voice and gesture we are
Challenged to make sense of where and what we find ourselves. No
Border guards patrol the Dyke, no frontier seals us in at Chepstow.
Did you really ever want that, John, seriously?
From here I have to question that stance. Were you quite as you
    appeared to be?
This locomotive worked the sidings in Cardiff and the junction,
Was scrapped at Barry and now is made to function
As an image of our hard-bitten history. *9629*, freshly painted green
    and black,
Her valves de-gutted, holds to her half-dozen yards of track:
No driver on the footplate, no steam, no destination,
This featureless hotel her final station,
Under the flags of Canada, Commerce and the Dragon.
I turn around. On the island in the Hayes a wino tilts his flagon
And light flashes from the moment.

III

SUMMER IN GREECE

Each day at noon the Englishman
drives into the sea.
He uses a seven-iron and places the balls
on a strip of carpet which he carries rolled
under his arm from the villa. A dozen
or two small splashes in the ocean.
They sink and cluster in the sand
gleaming like the hearts of opened sea-urchins.

Later, when it is cool, the boys swim out
and dive. They gather the balls —
Dunlop, Slazenger, Titleist, Penfold —
and return to the village. These are eggs
you can't crack or eat. They bounce.
There are no golf courses here.

Some mornings the Englishman from the villa
buys golf balls from the village.
They are cheap and the supply is constant.

POLES

An ancient woman in black
bends slowly over her row of beans.
The crop has come and gone and now
she pulls the yellow plants in bunches
out of the earth. She loosens
each pole of the row, then stretches to pull
the cross-stick which secures the length.
She works inch by inch,
a black shape against the shadows of the trees
and the whiteness of her ducks.
Passing down the road — Panzers, *Coca-Cola* trucks,
coaches of tourists. Beyond her plot
the sea in which we swim, from which we run
exhausted, tingling with salt, laughing.
Now she has raised the centre stick.
It balances on her finger tips like a javelin.
She lays it on the sheaf of spent poles
as they did at Thermopylae.

KALAVRYTA

Like a tattoo on the wrist — 13. 12. 43.
Those numerals underwrite everything.
This martyred town insists its destiny.

Under the square's ancient plane tree
The exasperated gauleiter fists in angry hectoring.
Like a tattoo on the wrist — 13. 12. 43.

All males over 15, step forward. Come with me!
Up the track to Kape's Hill forced marching
This martyred town insists its destiny.

His machine-gunners' calloused hands raked efficiently,
Their smoke and steam in the cold air engraving
Like a tattoo on the wrist — 13. 12. 43.

They bled the snow into icons of misery.
The hall clock's hands stuck at 2.34., unmoving.
This martyred town insists its destiny.

Now pines confer their summer cones, falling free
Around the close crypt, heady with candles' memories flaming.
Like a tattoo on the wrist — 13. 12. 43.
This martyred town insists its destiny.

Greece

WINDOW SEAT TO CHICAGO

Low cloud
banked over the western Atlantic
like arctic snow
puffed and ridged so
that if a bear should blunder
across it on all fours
I'd smile down,
watch it move on its belly,
fur-flop over the edge
into icy water.

Imagine the fur swept back swim-sleek
and the paws stretching and heaving through,
its snout conning the surface
and the eyes narrowed, the claws sprung
by an ache in the belly.

A whale's shadow cuts the horizon
before the whaler's prow
mushrooms out its harpoon
and crashes the dream.

WITNESS

The times I reckon best
is when the Lord really
take Hughie
and he feel the Lord
in his marrow and
the bones in him grind
against the presence
of the Lord
like He filin Hughie down
to a cuttin edge.
There ain't a thing you seen
like our Saviour workin
through that brother's body.

Nights at the temple you gets singin
to lift the roof so's that place
which ain't nothing but a shack
grows mighty as any city church.

With the singin done
may come a sister baptised
in the waters of God.
So we get to witnesses
and them as feels the spirit
proceed to Hughie
carryin it out to him in voices.
— all the Lord's voices.

And then if th' Almighty spirit
move the man greatly
on those nights Hughie calls

for the box
and he takes the key from around his neck
and opens that thing right up
and all the singin and swayin goes hush
when he go right in there with his hand
drawin out a copperhead or a rattler maybe.
All the time his eyes closed
him standin
there with the creature in his arms
windin up his shoulder
and twistin roun his neck.
Hughie wear the serpent like
our Lord made that slime into
the cross itself.

They shall take up serpents
and if they drink any deadly thing
it shall not hurt them . . .

Those nights I'm sayin
the folks feel lifted
they flyin home
the air thick as curd.
The Lord hangs heavy
in the trees
with their cares
His blood run fast
in the creek.
I casts off my shoes and cut
across the hill
walkin on stones.

I lay myself down
under His body nailed by the stars
alongside that she-moon
and His spirit tongue me
as I lie
His serpent grow in my hand.

BARRY ISLAND DREAM

(molto allegro)

The sun shone with a burnished gold sheen,
the waves curled like corn flakes.
Bank Holiday Monday was the scene.
She came from Splott —
everyone's dream, free and 16,
Queen of the canteen.
He was a plumber from Ponty —
he knew the lot.
They met in the funfair, taking
the air, not a care. Played
the machines, candy floss and screams,
Big Dipper dipped, waltzers waltzed
to make you sick. They sat at the back
of the Pirate Ship that swung
like the pendulum from Edgar Allan Poe.
She closed her eyes until it began
to slow. He held her tight —
she loved it. His left hand
slid over her woolly tit.
He brushed her lips with his,
sported the beginnings of a moustache.
She was tickled pink — he seemed keen
and had the cash. What a fling — why not?
In the House of Mirrors they bent
and hugged, knees splayed, lusty
and melting under lights. He puffed
up his chest like The Incredible Hulk.
She was creaming her tights. He bought
her a hat with "I'm the One".
She didn't care if it was love

or sex or just fun with a stranger.
His catch-phrase was "No danger".
In the Wacky Gold Mine he unbuttoned
his keks. The truck they rode in lurched
and clattered. Long before the end
the plumber looked shattered.
The sun was falling into the West,
her coach was leaving with the rest.
He offered to drive her in his van —
she said: "I can't." He said: "You can."
They played around in the Los Vegas Arcade —
Quick Draw — Grand Prix — Space Invaders —
Tried for a ring with mechanical arms,
she'd have settled for a bracelet with lucky charms.
The grab caught on air and nothing came.
No luck.
He said: "Fuck it — what a lark!"
I thought: Eat your heart out
John Cooper Clarke.

BREAKING SURFACE

Out of the oiled water
weeks later, they hoisted you, lovers
married in the cold depths of the docks.
And until the dredger's knock
and buckle against your car's roof,
they'd fictioned your runaway.
A sinful flight, snatched love in rented rooms,
incognito, with the scant luggage of a shame
friends and family presumed,
the strange newnesses they'd envied.
The loved, abandoned children calling your name.

Questions rise,
bubble and break the surface:
how was the bond made?
And where? Why
into the docks, such
grim and botched waters?
And what words, sucked
from the last air
before the rush of dark.
Such probings, metallic and cold.
Cold the kiss, the deepening cries.

Our comings and goings, trade
on the slop of water, wash over,
tread down such detritus as you.
The Sunday boys cast their bait
across the length of afternoon.
The weights find bottom and anchor.
Their lines crease the slick.

Nothing pulls.
No sound but the slapping sound
of stale trapped water.
Maybe drowned is best left drowned.

THE EMERALD

I stayed at the palace for the last three days
where he lay on a great bed
with its four pillars of solid silver shaped
as four naked women holding *punkahs*.

At the end they lifted him down and laid him
on a simple mat of straw and grasses —
from the level earth a man rises to greatness
and at the last the greatest of such will return

to a common ground.
As his final breath escaped there
came a noise such as I had never heard
nor wish again to hear.

The women's cries, rising to a wail,
an eerie keening that cut
through the endless passages of that place.
This is the very sound of death, I thought.

In leaving I passed their room
and finding the door ajar, I entered
for the first and only time
that private place — *zenana*.

The Maharanees were entranced and swayed
in the wake of their wailing.
I took a step inside and felt myself losing
my feet — the floor was treacherously aflame!

Encrusted like a carpet in a fable —
for it is the Hindu way that women let fall
their jewels to the ground in loss.
A king's ransom lay there, stopped short of his soul.

Filling the pockets of my suit
would have bought me a title back
here in England. I stooped
once. A large emerald.

My last wish is — keep this
as the memory of my years in India.
This alone is for you and your daughters
after you from my time in the service.

Wear it clear and public on your
breasts. A stolen thing, a remembrance.
We British, we are
a people beyond the humility of straw.

AT OCHRID LAKE

for Zoran Anchevski

After the monastery of Sveta Naum,
after the frescoes and the blank spaces
of the stolen frescoes,
after the poems and cameras
and the sound-crew man who played for us
James Taylor on his guitar, we swim
beneath the mountains
in the lake's shallow warmth,
feet curling over the smooth, muddy pebbles.

Around the headland Albania's
border-posts, visa checks, the guard's cold eyes.
Across the lake are the blue-distant Greek hills.
Macedonia wedged into the Balkans —
tyrannized, subjugated, partitioned
by Greeks, Serbs, Bulgars, Turks, Nazis,
the Austro-Hungarian Empire,
century after century.

Zoran, once you climbed in these mountains
to find still the scars of the Great War —
shallow trenches cut into the rocks,
brambles of wire, shells, skulls
bleached white like great birds' eggs.

Beneath the hills
from the shadowed groves at our backs
pure water springs from the ground,
gathers into a river that courses
a current clear through the lake.

As we wade from the shallows
further into the flow, the river hits
us like a wall of cold. Suddenly
icy the water's caress turns
to manacles locked around our legs —
it is like the promise of death, then
under this faultless sky,
like death itself.

FROM THE CITY THAT SHONE

The thing we dreamt of most was a bath:
so we crossed the wire and made for Gonnelieu
where, it was said, a tin bath lay abandoned
near the well of the convent school.
We kept to ruined shadows down the street,
towels and soap in our haversacks.

John had a canvas bucket and filled it from the well.
The bath held firm, the water cold and sweet.
I lorded it there in the weedy garden
amidst the ransacked books strewn all about,
broken glass wicked in the sun,
then towelled dry while
John tipped the water across the grass.

I drew fresh water for him and passed the soap.
"I always sing," he said.
"Too risky," I said.
But he splashed and hummed
— *And who shall kiss her ruby lips*
When I am far away? —

I sat on the path, my hair drying,
my head thrown back to the clearing sky
where a Taube stuttered through clouds from the West.
In those moments before the guns started up
it seemed that summer was held in place.

John rose from the water
"Like a god," he said,
his arms outstretched, then lobbed the soap

grenade-like at my head.
It squirted past me, diving in the slips.

We dressed
— each stuck a dog-rose in his tunic —
and turned back to our trenches.
Pressed into the shadows, I thought:
What does this all mean?

Two young soldiers, for a moment
Sunday-school clean in all this mess.
The Taube crossed overhead, coughing smoke,
and made desperate way to his own lines.

THE LAST CANDLES

The final stage of our journey over
we reached Odessa. So glorious
a scene I think my eyes had never taken in —
the harbour bristling with ships of all the allied nations.
We were received at the consulate by a young man,
fresh and clean in a crisp English suit.
Courteous and gentlemanly. I had not seen
such a man for three years.

In the hotel that night my dreams were of uniforms
and wounds, but one wound served for many —
thus, a severed arm at Biyech, the lacerated
stomach of a boy in Khutanova, the bloody head
of a captured Turk in Noscov — and then swabs
fell like the first snows of Winter,
the land chill and beyond pain
under its bandages.

For breakfast we were offered white bread and an egg!
The smell of coffee made me dizzy.

At nine we leave for the harbour. The streets
packed with aimless crowds, though everything
makes way for the *Bolsheviki* in their lorries.
At the harbour gates a man of no apparent rank
holds our papers for an hour.
He has a rifle and a long knife hangs
from his belt. A red band has been clumsily
sewn to the sleeve of his coat.

Some of the Norwegian crew speak English.
My cabin proves small, but warm.
After years under canvas, sheltering in ruins,
nursing beneath shattered roofs,
I am glad to call it home.
Though the place is strange and metallic
after stone and wood and earth.

Doctor Rakhil calls to take me on deck
for our departure.
                Ten years of living in this great land
have brought me to love it.
Though three of those years have been spent in war,
and then this anarchy, this revolution.
I see Odessa under red flags
as we cast off and the engines churn.
I feel everything moving away from me
as if Russia were a carpet being rolled to the sky.
At the harbour mouth Doctor Rakhil
gently turns me from the rail,
but is not quite quick enough.

That night, the sea pressing around me,
I dream of three things —
                    a day
in Moscow, when Nadya and I
were close enough to reach out and touch
the Tsar, and an old peasant
who had crawled through the crowd, between
the legs of the guards, clutching
his ragged petition,

still calling out as their boots struck him.
Nicholas II, Tsar of all the Russias, flickered
his eyes, but his step was the unfaltering
step of a god.
                My first dead man
in the training ward. Grey and small in the candlelight,
his mouth like a closed purse and what seemed
to be butterflies on his face. Two sugarlumps
to weigh down his eye-lids.
                        And at last, this leaving
Odessa. How in the shadows I saw them —
officers from the front fleeing the chaos of desertion
and caught by the Reds at the port.
They bound their feet to heavy stones
and planted them in the harbour. Swaying, grey shapes
I glimpsed from the rail, as if
bowing to me.
The last candles of my Russia
guttering and going out under the black sea.

FRIEDHOF

They are tending the dead at Ypres.
The beech leaves, November bronze,
are lifted and rolled over
into rows between the slabs
by the gardener's blower
while three others follow to rake
the long mound and fork
this harvest into their barrows.

Behind the barbs of squared beech hedge
each yard of peace names its German dead,
twenty by twenty on dark, flat slabs
so that, without the steady sweepers,
you might come to this place as to a park,
tread the leaves in a path to the two figures
— a man, a woman; a father, a mother,
kneeling sharp and hunched before
some undetermined loss.

Years after the war, Kathe Kollwitz,
finding at last her only son's grave,
shaped these two from stone.
Now, his wooden cross a museum piece,
his name is flattened with the others
under this brief quilt of leaves.

At Tyn Cot, The New Irish Farm,
St Julien Dressing Station,
at Sanctuary Wood, at Lijssenthoek,
and a hundred cemeteries more,
the victorious dead, white-stoned, upright,

are ranked in the democracy of death —
Dorset, Welch, Highlander, Sikh,
Six men of the Chinese Labour Force.
The whole world bled through Flanders.

Turning the wet earth, Flemish farmers
still find wire and bones
tangled with the potatoes and beet.
And, occasionally, the local paper
carries at the bottom of a page —
Farmer blinded by shell.
It happens when they remove the detonator
from the rusty casing. The trade is well
established. The explosive is tired
but has a pedigree right enough for the men
of Armagh, Fermanagh, Crossmaglen.

HOME FRONT

That winter of our Island Fortress,
the docks blacked-out and sirens wailing,
the house closed its brittle silence around her.
Rain drummed the windows behind her children's dreams
Over the months she saved from her widow's pay
and the hours of cleaning at the manse
seven silver coins, one from the abdication year
with the head of the love-lost king.

Should the coastline be split by incoming shells,
parachutes flower in the Vale
and jackboots strut in King's Square,
then she would lay her six children
to sleep, sealing the windows and doors
with newspapers and blankets.
Seven shillings' worth of gas
would deliver them out of occupation.

For months she has dreamt of his lost freighter,
torpedoed six days out of New York,
men overboard, gagging on salt and diesel.
How the ship reared and plunged like a whale,
her wash sweeping cold hands from flotsam.
As he sank into the anonymous dark
the final waves from her
minting coins from the constant moon.

Tonight the City of London burns
with St Paul's untouched at the very centre.
At the edge of night the Welsh ports sound no alarms.
She opens the curtains to a moon-bright sky,

counts out the coins in the tea-caddy
and holds them, cupped in her palms.
OMN. REX Defender of the Faith. Emperor of India.
The seven polished shillings sing in her hands.

COUPLES FROM THE FIFTIES

Vague shapes stiff and grey all those miles away
The Coronation in our front-room — dull monotype, limited edition.

*

I smelt the Alvis's leather back seat as my father's radio declared
War on Egypt — the Suez route to India, East of Anthony Eden.

*

Mau Mau, Eoka, National Service, Singapore, Berlin.
The war won, the Empire dimming, the curtains coming down.

*

Rock 'n' Roll came to Carmarthen, two years late — the usherettes
Amazed as kids jived in the *Lyric's* aisles, just like the *Fathé News*

*

Buddy, Elvis, Cliff, Gene, the original Comets and Bill.
The sweetest love-song ya ever heard — Don and Phil.

*

The outcasts, the lunch-time loners, the misunderstood,
We trekked to the lost geyser springs of Fecci's espresso.

*

Coffee steam blends with Woodbine smoke and through it all
The Mekon juke-box doing slow-motion card tricks.

*

In Blackpool I held out my autograph book for David Nixon — in
    colour!
Who made cards machine-gun, vanish, then float back into view like
    gulls.

*

Dad's challenge — up the Lynton hill in the little black Austin, first
    gear:
Then back down on the brake to what the sea had left of the sea-wall,
    Lynmouth.

*

In the grey-dark matinees of the *Lyric* I plundered
The idea of oysters in a coral reef of petticoats.

HOTEL CARMARTHEN

This lank-haired woman
bare-foot at breakfast talks
of searching for a house
while her five-year-old pulls faces, pulls
clothes, tramples feet at the other tables.

*My daddy is married to Sarah now and
she's had a baby and we are moving here
to live and you can't guess my name —
it's Layla.*

Ah, yes, *Eric Clapton*, I say.
*I myself was born here,
but why have you and your daughter . . .
I mean, why Carmarthen?*

*For Llanpumpsaint,
the Temple.
It's a community —
the community of the many names of God.
They have an elephant,
don't they, Layla?
I meditate.
    Though I find
the Welsh themselves
are so closed and unfriendly,
just like the people in the Shetlands.*

My knife scrapes across the toast.
— *Really? But the Valleys,
you can't have lived in the Valleys.*

Oh, yes, we've spent time in Tregaron,
that's a valley.

Thirty years ago, I cast off
Carmarthen like tired, dated clothes.
The world was louder, brighter, elsewhere.
Now there's incense, antiques, sandals
and pulses in the market,
buskers in the streets.

And in the hand-me-down hills, smoke
rises again. Runes are disclosed
in the mud of the lanes,
tractors scratch at the edge
of a dawn mantra.

Layla, perched in the tree, cradles
a discovered nest, then
empties it into the sky.

TO ARTHUR

Gwilym wedged up a sand storm in the jumping pit
and emptied the bunker of his imagination
while you smiled wryly and saw that the lads
sent to chuck spears at the other end of the rugby field
didn't spill blood at another Rorke's Drift.

He was always the manic, serious sportsman,
ex-international centre, buffeting through our flailing
arms to ghost towards the memory of Stradey tries,
lofting again and again
that sweet dropped goal at Lansdowne Road.

Golf struck him like a tumour, blowing up to football size,
leaving little room for work: Form Two Gym became monkeyings
from the ropes and wallbars while he endlessly adjusted his grip
to waft plastic balls off the coconut matting towards
the 18th green, tucked testingly in behind the horse.

But out on the course it is you I remember,
walking the links familiarly as your back garden,
flighting the ball knowingly into the wind, drifting it
between and off the cruel slopes of dune
to settle on those desert islands of green.

Your swing was your essence — calm,
unhurried, a deliberate wind-back from the tee
to cock at the notched point over your left shoulder.
Then the unwinding of the arc to stroke the ball
with a power won from timing rather than exertion.

Always the backdrop of beach and sea and Caldey Island
with the weather coming clear across the Atlantic.
The waves' roar lost in the wind or holiday scream,
but glinting there, again and again, like the life-beats your heart
now pumps with deliberation across the hospital screen.

Though a bandit's laid you low up there in Haverfordwest,
Arthur, be sustained by our thoughts, the generations
of kids who scrummed and drove and tackled their best.
This third-rate hooker and the rest refuse to believe
Time could do what the Luftwaffe and Tenby links could not
    achieve.

TRAIN JOURNEY: TRIANGLES

That glorious run from Carmarthen,
the line clinging to the banks
of the river along
the salty pastures and mud flats.

The Towy blessed by a wash
of late afternoon sun —
March softening the hint
of an evening chill.

The tide has ebbed beyond the castle
of Llanstephan. Waders, gulls
a pair of curlew strut and dab
in the shallows and rills.

Past Glanfferri we curve
south and east around the bay
towards Swansea — a caravan park,
a power station, the leavings of industry.

*

The coach empties and fills again at Swansea.
Opposite me a man sits down — perhaps five years
further into his forties, balding,
moustached, pale with thin glasses.
He settles his shoulder against the window
and unfolds his copy of *Gay Times*.
On the cover a beautiful young man
thigh-deep in the sea flexes
and pulls at his skin-tight t-shirt.
It is a version of *Penthouse*.

The off-duty driver across from him
immediately rises and moves to another carriage.
Our fellow travellers raise their faces, stiffen,
draw in a single breath.

I remember that the King of Denmark in the war
a happy, family man, sickened
by the slaughtering prejudice, had sewn
to all his public clothes the *Juden's* yellow star
and wore it through the Occupation.
As I recall the story, no-one wore
in protest the Nazi's pink triangle for queers.

At Port Talbot two schoolboys peer in, point
and smirk through the window.
The train casts off more passengers
at Neath, Bridgend and then
we slice steadily into the Vale
of Glamorgan with the light
failing across a muted landscape
that unfolds into Cardiff's suburbs.
Long after his eyes must have strained for the print,
our gay resolutely scans
the proclamation of his raised pages.

At Cardiff Central he is the first to leave,
his magazine folded into a tapestry shoulder-bag.
He walks ahead of us
lightly along the platform
and disappears down the stairway
into what we all acknowledge as night.

AFTER SKOPJE

for Zoran Anchevski

You still wake, sweating from the nightmare of it.
At the station to meet your uncle
when the ceiling shook and flaked apart
snowing plaster and cracking like a branch.
One of the soldiers grabbed you up,
half pulled, half carried you outside.

Dumped and dazed on the quaking pavement
you watched amazed as he ran back
through the door to his fellows.
And as he passed through the shadowed arch
the whole station collapsed on them
as if the city had taken in a great breath.

A thunder
then the echo of thunder.
Dust clogging your eyes and throat.
You sleepwalked home —
a hand, an arm, legs
still-born from the rubble.

Here in the south as you bathe in the lake,
you always make for weeds on the river bed
that the water strokes, remembering
the hair that grew from beneath a wall,
hair that stirred as you ran to your home,
to what in the dream is always sunlit and calm.

Until you split the walls with your cries —
Mami! Dado!

You remember your father's tears like a river,
your mother's swaying embrace
like a deep current holding you,
carrying you on.

THE TREBLE

His voice came to us
like a fine glass ringing,
a memory high and clear as sky
through the summits of a windy tree
claimed by a boy on the first
real day of Spring

who, throwing his head back, bathes
in cloud and treads the air.
Think of the dolphin's curved note,
the moonlit blade of a wave,
the hard, innocent sparkle of frost.
This is the way we imagine angels.

And then it broke.
After a fevered night his dream pulled
him through caverns that spat back echoes,
his voice quavered and roughened when he woke,
a silting of the throat. And the song
weighed full of grit, cracked and sank.

Shaving now in the bathroom mirror
his father's blade smoothing over the adam's apple
snicks tracers of blood at his neck.
He presses his face into the arms of a towel,
feels the strange fingers of another
soothing his wounded throat,

rubbing from the hardened chest,
drumming over the face's soft mask
to the roots of his scalp.

Those woman's hands in his towel
playing out the older song beneath
that was always there to be sung.

SECOND HALF

Three-nil down
and the wind to come
in our faces
for the second half.

The ball's barely
gone to hand —
we've kicked it
all away.

Warm scotch
in a cold, snug hipflask.
The sour end of the season
sweetens on the tongue.

My father would have
cheered and cheered
to make believe
in this match.

Next year, son,
big enough, you'll come
circled in my arms
from the crush.

We'll move into the crowd.
I'll learn to ease my hold.
Later, swept apart,
we'll spill out into the street.

Acknowledgements

Confrontation, Mississippi Valley Review, New England Review & Bread Loaf Quarterly, The Kenyon Review, The New Welsh Review, Poetry Wales, Planet, Poetry Review, Prospice, The Reaper, The Times Literary Supplement, 2+2, Verse.

The Observer/ Arvon 1985 Anthology ed. Clampitt, Raine, Stevenson: Arvon.
P.E.N. Anthology 1989 ed. Elaine Feinstein: Quartet Books.
The Poetry Book Society Anthology 1986/87 ed. Jonathan Barker: Hutchinson.
A Cardiff Anthology ed. Meic Stephens: Seren Books.
The Poetry Book Society Anthology 1987/88 ed. Gillian Clarke: Hutchinson.
First and Always: The Great Ormond Street Anthology ed. Lawrence Sail: Faber & Faber.

'Friedhof' was broadcast on *Poetry Now* BBC Radio 3.
'Macquette' was published in *Le Poet et son Lecteur* ed. Eugene van Itterbeck.

Four poems were included in *Poems — Selected & New*, Story Line Press, California, 1986. Two are reprinted, with emendations from my *Selected Poems 1970–85* Poetry Wales Press, 1986.
'From the City that Shone' — the title and story idea came from the autobiography of V. de Sola Pinto.
 'The Last Candles' — the story idea came from *A Nurse on the Russian Front 1914-1918* by Florence Farnborough.